Hemingway's Articles for the Kansas City Star

Ernest Hemingway

Hemingway's articles for the Kansas City Star

Hemingway was employed by the Kansas City Star from October 17/18 1917 through the end of April 1918.

CONTENTS

- Kerensky, The Fighting Flea
- Battle of Raid Squads
- At the End of the Ambulance Run
- Throng at Smallpox Case
- Laundry Car over Cliff
- Six Men Become Tankers
- Big Day for Navy Drive
- Navy Desk Jobs to Go
- Would 'Treat 'em Rough'
- Recruits for the Tanks
- Daredevil Joins Tanks
- Mix War, Art and Dancing

Hemingway's Articles for the Kansas City Star

Kerensky, The Fighting Flea

Somehow, although he is the smallest office boy around the place, none of the other lads pick on him. Scuffling and fighting almost has ceased since Kerensky came to work. That's only one of the nicknames of Leo Kobreen, and was assigned to him because of a considerable facial resemblance to the perpetually fleeing Russian statesman, and, too, because both wore quite formal standing collars.

In size, Leo is about right for spanking. But that never will happen to Leo. Although he is inches short of five feet, there is a bulkiness about his shoulders that gains respect even from those Cossacks of the business world, the messenger boys.

In fact, it was a messenger, coming in blusteringly, who first made it known that Leo possessed a reputation. Almost politely the cocky young fellow handed a yellow envelope to the office bantam.

"Why it's Kid Williams," he said, "Are you going to fight at the club Saturday night, Kid?"

"I should have known it," the boss said, "Kerensky has all the characteristics of a prize fighter. After a short round of work doesn't he retire to a corner and sit down?"

Then some of them remembered Kid Williams in preliminary bouts...One of those boys who scrap three rounds before the big fighters enter the ring. That's Kerensky.

You may have thrown some loose change into the ring at the final gong. How you laughed to see the two bantams push each other about and scramble fiercely each to pick up the most. Sometimes they couldn't wait to get their gloves off. All the fight fans roared at them trying to pick up thin dimes in their padded fists.

"That's all hippodrome stuff," Kerensky says. "The men like to see us quarrel over the money, but win or lose, we split it fifty-fifty. My half of the pickup runs form $1.50 to $2.50."

The worst thing about the fight game, take it from Kerensky, is the smoke. He has even considered retiring from the ring because it is so upsetting to take a deep breath of tobacco fumes.

"But of course I haven't quit," he explains. "Right now if I knew some of the clubs downtown had a smoker on and they offered me $2, of course I'd get in and fight."

How would Kerensky advise a young man to open a pugilistic career? Well, he just picked up his skill. For several years he sold papers, and you know how one thing leads to another. There is a newsboy rule that if one boy installs himself on a corner no ot her can sell there. A full grown man used to cry the headlines on a certain Grand Avenue crossing. Poachers bothered him.

"It wouldn't look right for a big fellow to hit a little kid," says Kerensky, "so he let me sell there, too, and sicked me on all the strange boys. I always ran them away. He liked me and called me Kid Williams, after the bantamweight champion."

Kerensky's last street fight was to a big gate. A newsboy of larger growth was the victim. They clinched and fell to the sidewalk. A crowd gathered, but the crossing patrolman turned his back till the battle was over. Then he came over and said: "Leo, I guess you'll have to cut this out."

After that, when Leo wanted to fight, somebody had to hire a hall. He began going into the gymnasiums to sell papers. There he watched the big men train for their Convention Hall bouts. Sometimes the proprietors would let him come in and work out beside Thorpe or Chavez for nothing. It costs the ordinary citizen a dime, Leo says, to get in and work at the pulleys and weights at times like these.

His opportunity came to go on in a newsboy bout at a smoker in Cutler's gymnasium. The kid glows yet at the mention of that bout.

"It was the best fight of my career," he says. "I went in mad, and gave the fans their money's worth. But I was awful green, and was almost knocked out in the last round. Now I know how to study 'em, and I don't have to work as hard."

After hard days in old Russia, the life is full of joy for Leo, and who can say that he is not making the most of his opportunities? When he talks of the past it is of a program. That Christmas season the workmen in a sugar refinery near Kiev made a cross of ice and set it up on the frozen river. It fell over and they blamed the Jews. Then the workmen rioted, breaking into stores and smashing windows. Leo and his family hid on the roof for three days, and his sister fell ill of pneumonia. One studies to change the subject and asks:

"Leo, do they ever match you with a bigger boy?"

"Oh no," he says, "the crowd wouldn't stand for that. But sometimes I catch one on the street."

Battle of Raid Squads

John M. Tully and Albert Raithel, revenue officers from St. Louis, may die, and two city detectives narrowly escaped injury as a result of a revolver battle yesterday through a case of mistaken identity.

Tully and Raithel ha d gone to raid a house at 2743 Mercier street, reported to be a rendezvous for drug users. Edward Kritser and Paul Conrad, city detectives, arrived a few minutes later on the same mission. Each party of officers mistook the other for drug peddlers.

Tully was shot in the right leg, left arm and lower abdomen. Raithel was wounded in the abdomen and left wrist. Both will recover. The two detectives were uninjured, but both had bullet holes through their clothing.

The wounded men were taken to the General Hospital. Later they were removed to the Swedish Hospital.

While on the surface the shooting of the two government officers appeared to be a case of mistaken identity, elements of a mysterious nature which Francis M. Wilson, United States district attorney, refused to make public, crept into the case last night.

At 11 o'clock last night the district attorney took a statement from Tully. He said he could not disclose its contents. It was admitted by another government official there was "something back of the whole affair."

It was said all of the evidence with regard to the shooting and developments leading to the affair will be placed before Hunt C. Moore, prosecutor. Senator Wilson said the government would co-operate with the prosecutor. The district attorney conferred two hours last night with Chief Flahive and John Halpin, police commissioner. At the close Senator Wilson said he felt certain the prosecuting attorney would do his duty in the case.

Tully gave this story of the shooting:

"Raithel and I received information that there was a nest of drug addicts at a house at 2743 Mercier Street. We secured a search warrant from S.O. Hargis, assistant United States district attorney, and went out. In the house was an old woman. We ques tioned her and could learn nothing, so left to watch the house and question a few of the neighbors. We were standing across the street when a motor car drove up and two men and a girl got out. One of the men carried a handbag. Raithel and I thought they were `dope heads.' I w ent to the front door and Raithel to the rear. Inside the door I saw Bernie Lamar's girl. She said, `Hello Jack.' Then a man stepped out of the next room. I walked up to him and touched him on the shoulder, saying, `Hold on a minute, I'm an officer.' Then he started shooting. He got me in the arm. I shot twice and then got out the door. I got across the street and fell in front of a house. Then the other man shot me again. I emptied my revolver and then staggered over to a garage acro ss the road."

Raithel was operated on as soon as he was taken to the hospital and was unable to make a statement.

The two detectives told a different story. According to them the battle was the culmination of a feud between a gang of drug addicts and government agents.

About seven months ago Bernard Abe, a notorious police character, was sent to the Fort Leavenworth prison for drug peddling. John Tully had secured the evidence that convicted Aberer. His wife, Rose Aberer, alias Rose Fuqua, known as Rose Lamar, has been living here with a man named William "Irish" Rogers, also a drug addict and holder of a police record. When Tully arrested Aberer the government secured a large quantity of narcotics. Lately the federal officials here have been trailing Rose Fuqua, trying to locate the rest of the big supply of drugs which she was believed to have hidden. Two special agents were sent from the St. Louis office to aid in the work.

Friday night Rose Fuqua and Williams were shadowed to the Stratford Hotel, 616 East Eighth Street, where they registered as Mr. and Mrs. William Sullivan. Yesterday the revenue office obtained two detectives from police headquarters to aid in raiding the room at the Stratford. Kritser and Conrad were assigned. Rose, a man named Richard C. Adams, and Rogers were arrested in the room and a quantity of narcotics found. The woman confessed to the government agents that the missing drugs were hidden in her mother's home at 2743 Mercier Street. The city detectives took her and Rodgers out to the address.

Conrad and Kritzer found a sack containing a quantity of heroin, morphine, opium and two complete "hop smoking" outfits hidden in the house. Conrad says he was talking to Rose Fuqua in the front room of the 5-room frame house when he heard a knock o n the door. A man entered. The woman said, "Hello, Jack, how are you?" Conrad said in a sworn statement.

"I concluded from the familiar way he spoke to her that he was a member of the gang," the detective said. "The man turned to me and said 'Who are you?' reached for his revolver and reached for my shoulder. I drew my revolver and fired twice. He sho t at me three times. One bullet went through my coat, another grazed the side of my face. My shot struck him and he reeled out of the front door. Another man (Raithel) shot at me through the window. I fired three times and then went behind a door to reload my gun.

"I heard someone shooting in the rear of the house and saw Kritser shooting at a man across the street. I stepped around and exchanged shots with a man shooting from behind a grocery wagon. I thought we were fighting a gang of dope fiends and rushed to the next house on the north, firing as I went. Kritser and I both shot at a man firing across the street. The small man dropped. Someone yelled, 'They're government men.' We stopped firing.

Neither one of them said anything about being officers to me."

Kritser's story and that told by Rose Fuqua agreed with Conrad's. Rose Fuqua and Rogers escaped in the fight, but later gave themselves up.

Buddie, a dog owned by Rogers, was shot in the leg and is being taken care of by a neighbor. Adams, Rogers, and Rose Fuqua are being held at police headquarters for investigation.

At the End of the Ambulance Run

The night ambulance attendants shuffled down the long, dark corridors at the General Hospital with an inert burden on the stretcher. They turned in at the receiving ward and lifted the unconscious man to the operating table. His hands were calloused and he was unkempt and ragged, a victim of a street brawl near the city market. No one knew who he was, but a receipt, bearing the name of George Anderson, for $10 paid on a home out in a little Nebraska town served to identify him.

The surgeon opened the swollen eyelids. The eyes were turned to the left. "A fracture on the left side of the skull," he said to the attendants who stood about the table. "Well, George, you're not going to finish paying for that home of yours."

"George" merely lifted a hand as though groping for something. Attendants hurriedly caught hold of him to keep him from rolling from the table. But he scratched his face in a tired, resigned way that seemed almost ridiculous, and placed his hand ag ain at his side. Four hours later he died.

It was merely one of the many cases that come to the city dispensary from night to night — and from day to day for that matter; but the night shift, perhaps, has a wider range of the life and death tragedy — and even comedy, of the city. When "Geo rge" comes in on the soiled, bloody stretcher and the rags are stripped off and his naked, broken body lies on the white table in the glare of the surgeon's light, and he dangles on a little thread of life, while the physicians struggle grimly, it is all in the night's work, whether the thread snaps or whether it holds so that George can fight on and work and play.

Here comes another case. This time a small man limps in, supported by an ambulance man and a big policeman in uniform. "Yes, sir, we got a real robber this time — a real one — just look at him!" the big officer smiled. "He tried to hold up a dru g store, and the clerks slipped one over on him. It was a—"

"Yes, but they was three of 'em, an' they was shootin' all at once," the prisoner explained. Since there was no use in attempting to deny the attempted robbery, he felt justified in offering an alibi for his frustrated prowess. "It looks like I oug htta got one of 'em, but then, maybe, I'll do better next time.

"Say, you'd better hurry up and get these clothes off of me, before they get all bloody. I don't want 'em spoiled." He was thoroughly defeated and dejected, and the red handkerchief he used for a mask still hung from his neck.

He rolled a cigarette, and as the attendants removed his clothes, a ball of lead rattled to the floor. "Whee! It went clear through, didn't it? Say, I'll be out before long, won't I, doc?"

"Yes — out of the hospital," the physician replied significantly.

Out on Twenty-seventh street a drug clerk — the one of the three who used the .38 — has a .38 bullet dangling from his watch chain.

* *

One night they brought in a negro who had been cut with a razor. It is not a mere joke about negroes using the razor — they really do it. The lower end of the man's heart had been cut away and there was not much hope for him.

Surgeons informed his relatives of the one chance that remained, and it was a very slim one. They took some stitches in his heart and the next day he had improved sufficiently to be seen by a police sergeant.

"It was just a friend of mine, boss," the negro replied weakly to questioning. The sergeant threatened and cajoled, but the negro would not tell who cut him. "Well, just stay there and die, then," the officer turned away exasperated.

But the negro did not die. He was out in a few weeks, and the police finally learned who his assailant was. He was found dead — his vitals opened by a razor.

"It's razor wounds in the African belt and slugging in the wet block. In Little Italy they prefer the sawed-off shotgun. We can almost tell what part of the city a man is from just by seeing how they did him up," one of the hospital attendants comme nted.

* *

But it is not all violence and sudden death that comes to the attention of the emergency physicians. They attend the injuries and ills of charity patients. Here is a laborer who burned his foot one morning when he used too much kerosene in building the fire, and over there is a small boy brought in by his mother, who explains there is something the matter with his nose. An instrument is inserted into the nostril of the squirming youngster and is drawn forth. A grain of corn, just sprouted, dangles at the end of the steel.

One day an aged printer, his hand swollen from blood poisoning, came in. Lead from the type metal had entered a small scratch. The surgeon told him they would have to amputate his left thumb.

"Why, doc? You don't mean it do you? Why, that'd be worsen sawing the periscope off of a submarine! I've just gotta have that thumb. I'm an old-time swift. I could set my six galleys a day in my time — that was before the linotypes came in. Even now , they need my business, for some of the finest work is done by hand.

And you go and take that finger away from me and — well, it'd mighty interesting to know how I'd ever hold a `stick' in my hand again. Why, doc! — "

With face drawn, and heard bowed, he limped out the doorway. The French artist who vowed to commit suicide if he lost his right hand in battle, might have understood the struggle the old man had alone in the darkness. Later that night the printer retu rned. He was very drunk.

"Just take the damn works, doc, take the whole damn works," he wept.

* *

At one time a man from out in Kansas, a fairly likable and respectable sort of man to look at him, went on a little debauch when he came to Kansas City. It was just a little incident that the folks in the home town would never learn about. The ambulance b rought him from a wine room, dead from a stroke of heart disease. At another time (it happens quite often) a young girl took poison. The physicians who saved her life seldom speak of the case. It she had died her story might have been told — but she has to live.

And so the work goes on. For one man it means a clean bed and prescriptions with whisky in it, possibly, and for another, it is a place in the potters' field. The skill of the surgeon is exercised just the same, no matter what the cause of the injury or t he deserts of the patient.

* *

The telephone bell is ringing again. "Yes, this the receiving ward," says the desk attendant. "No. 4 Police

Station, you say? A shooting scrape? All right they'll be right over." And the big car speeds down the Cherry Street hill, the headlights borin g a yellow funnel into the darkness.

Throng at Smallpox Case

While the chauffeur and male nurse on the city ambulance devoted to the carrying of smallpox cases drove from the General Hospital to the municipal garage on the North Side today to have engine trouble "fixed" a man, his face and hands covered with smallpox pustules, lay in one of the entrances to the Union Station. One hour and fifteen minutes after having been given the call the chauffeur and nurse reported at the hospital with the man, G.T. Brewer, 926 West Forty-second Street. The ambulance had been repaired.

Behind that vehicle was an ambulance from the Emergency Hospital, ordered to get the patient by Dr. James Tyree, in charge of contagious diseases, after repeated calls from the station.

Brewer, a life insurance agent, arrived from Cherryvale, Kas., this morning. At 9 o'clock James McManus, officer in charge of the police station at the depot, found him lying in the west entrance to the lobby. Streams of persons, hurrying past, eddied about Brewer while solicitous passersby asked the trouble. At 9:50 McManus placed a policeman near the sick man to keep persons away.

McManus says he called the contagious department of the hospital immediately after finding Brewer. An ambulance was promised. Two calls were sent the hospital later and each time, so McManus says, he was told the ambulance was on the way. Doctor Tyree once insisted McManus take the sick man into the police office there, but McManus refused, saying more persons would be exposed. Doctor Tyree also said the ambulance would be there "right away."

When the ambulance did reach the station at 10:15, the driver explained it had been broken down while out on another call.

Doctor Tyree explained later that the regular sick ambulance, No. 90, was wrecked last night. When the call first was received at the receiving ward of the General Hospital at 9:05 o'clock ambulance No. 92, the smallpox carrier, was dispatched, he sa id.

"But the ambulance had motor trouble," Doctor Tyree continued. "The chauffeur and the male nurse in charge decided to go to the municipal garage and get the trouble fixed."

The garage, on the North Side, is about as far from the hospital as the distance from the hospital to the Union Station and return.

Doctor Tyree criticized the police for failure to remove Brewer to an isolated place instead of leaving him "where scores of travelers came in contact and were exposed to smallpox."

Laundry Car over Cliff

Laundry strike sympathizers drove a Walker Laundry Company motor truck over Cliff Drive hill at Hardesty Avenue late this afternoon, after capturing the car and routing the driver and two special officers at Fourteenth Street and Euclid Avenue. One of the special officers fired a shot into the crowd before fleeing from the rain of bricks and stones. No one was injured.

Homer Maze, 5106 East Twenty-fourth Street, was driving the laundry truck. Guarding him were two special officers, Sam Seaman, 2700 East Twenty-seventh Street, and C.L. Winner, 717 East Eleventh Street.

Maze was making a delivery at Fourteenth street and Euclid Avenue when a crowd of about twenty-five man and women approached from the west and opened fire of rocks and stones on the standing car. Maze came from the house and made a run to join the sp ecial officers. After several minutes of fusillading stones, the officers and Maze deserted the car and reported the disturbance at the Flora Avenue Police Station. Seaman, one of the special officers, told of firing a shot toward the crowd, attempting to disperse the strike sympathizers. Re-enforcements joining the attacking party seemed to arrive steadily, they said, so they gave up the car to the crowed.

When the police arrived at the scene of the disturbance a part of the crowd was yet there. Six men and one woman were arrested. The men could not be identified by Maze or the special officers as having thrown stones. The woman, Julia Anderson, 1711 We st Prospect Place, was identified by them and was held on a $51 cash bond. She denies having thrown anything.

The truck was found after a search, but is practically demolished.

A second ``wrecking party *was reported from Eleventh Street and Chestnut Avenue. B. L. Ferguson, 6424 Lee Street, driver of a Kansas City Laundry Company truck, and a special officer, Salvator Schira, 1911 Missouri Avenue, were attacked by fifteen men and twelve women. A stone thrown by one of the striking laundry workers struck Ferguson on the cheek, another on the right hand. His injuries are not severe.*

Six Men Become Tankers

Six men were accepted today for the new tank corps by Lieut. Frank E. Cooter, who arrived from Washington yesterday to recruit men for the special service. The men were selected from a crowd of twenty that appeared at the army recruiting office at Twelfth Street and Grand Avenue today. Men of various occupations, from bookkeepers to motor operators, applied for service today. Those accepted are:

Elvin L. Loyd, 1711 Penn Street, a tractor driver.

Harold E. McEachron, Atlanta, Ga., a machinist.

Kenneth C. Dills, 3939 Agnes Avenue, stenographer.

Robert E. Watson, 1317 West Thirteenth Street, stenographer.

Albert F. Henne, 207 East Twelfth Street.

Lewis M. Dean, Chicago, Ill.

The men of the tank corps enlist in a dangerous branch of the service, but it is thrilling work and, like aviation, has long periods of rest and inactivity between the short, concentrated spells of action.

All the men taken were of draft age and were given a letter from Col. I.C. Welborn of the tank corps, authorizing any local board to immediately induct them into service.

A returned officer from the western front now training recruits at the national tank training camp at Gettysburg, Pa., tells the inside story of one of the land ships in action.

For several days the men prepare for the coming offensive. The tanks are brought up behind the first line trenches under cover of darkness and the crews crawl into the close, oily smelling steel shells. The machine gunners, artillerymen and engineers get into their cramped quarters, the commander crawls into his seat, the engines clatter and pound and the great steel monster clanks lumberingly forward. The commander is the brains and the eyes of the tank. He sits crouched close under the fore turret and has a view of the jumbled terrain of the battle field through a narrow slit. The engineer is the heart of the machine, for he changes the tank from a mere protection into a living, moving fighter.

The constant noise is the big thing in a tank attack. The Germans have no difficulty seeing the big machine as it wallows forward over the mud and a constant stream of machine gun bullets plays on the armour, seeking any crevice. The machine gun bullets do no harm except to cut the camouflage paint from the sides.

The tank lurches forward, climbs up, and then slides gently down like an otter on an ice slide. The guns are roaring inside and the machine guns making a steady typewriter clatter. Inside the tank the atmosphere becomes intolerable for want of fresh air and reeks with the smell of burnt oil, gas fumes, engine exhaust and gunpowder.

The crew inside work the guns while the constant clatter of bullets on the armour sounds like rain on a tin roof. Shells are bursting close to the tank, and a direct hit rocks the monster. But the tank hesitates only a moment and lumbers on. Barb wire is crunched, trenches crossed and machine gun parapets smothered into the mud.

Then a whistle blows, the rear door of the tank is opened and the men, covered with grease, their faces black with the smoke of the guns, crowd out of the narrow opening to cheer as the brown waves of the infantry sweep past. Then its back to barracks and rest.

"We want fighters for the tank service," said Lieutenant Cooter today. "Real men that want to see action. No mollycoddles need apply." Men from 18 to 40 years old are being enlisted at the army recruiting station, Twelfth Street and Grand Avenue. Men of nearly all mechanical trades may enlist if they pass the personal inspection and mental test given by Lieutenant Cooter.

Big Day for Navy Drive

The second day of the naval drive for recruits for immediate duty took sixty-one men into the recruiting office at Eighth and Walnut streets. Thirty-eight were accepted, the largest number enlisted any day this year. Men enlist ed were of all ratings, seventeen seamen, five firemen, two radio men, two hospital apprentices, five carpenter's mates and three painter's mates.

Carpenters and painters are offered special inducements to enroll in the Naval Reserve under the new pay schedule. Both are enlisted in three classes, first, second and third class carpenter's mates. Artisans must have at least three years' experience in their trades before they may qualify for any of the ratings. A third class carpenter's mate receives $41 a month, second class $46 and first class $52. Carpenters are given a separation allowance, clothing allowance, subsistence allowance and medical attention without extra charge.

Lieut. Ralph B. Campbell, in charge of the recruiting here, has compiled figures to show a third class carpenter, the lowest paid rating, receives the equivalent of $150 a month. Reservists now are being sent to the Great Lakes Training Station as fas t as they are enlisted. Fifty left last night. Radio reserve men are under command of Commandant Moffett of Great Lakes and are being called alphabetically. The letter S was reached in the call today.

Navy Desk Jobs to Go

There will be no more desk warriors of draft age in the naval reserve as soon as an order issued by the bureau of navigation this morning goes into effect. By the order, all naval reservists of draft age who have had six months' training are at once ordered to sea duty unless they are physically disqualified. Reservists on recruiting duty, holding publicity jobs, doing any inland work, must leave at once for sea service.

Eight men will be lost from the naval recruiting station at Eighth and Walnut streets by the new order, Lieut. Ralph Campbell, head of naval recruiting here, said today.

Marguerite Clark, motion picture idol, who recently enrolled as a yeowoman in the naval reserve, will not be affected by the order, Lieutenant Campbell said, as it has not yet been extended to women.

The Great Lakes station has been called on to furnish a quota of six men a week to be sent to the engineer officers' section of the officers' material school at Pelham Bay Park, N.Y. Men enrolling in the reserve now will have a chance to qualify for the technical instruction at Pelham Bay. Men completing the course are commissioned ensigns and made junior deck officers.

Men now taking a course in technical school may enroll in the reserve to be sent to the Pelham Bay school on the completion of their college work. Eight students from the Kansas State Agricultural College arrived here today to enroll in the reserve for officers material. Four are in the junior class and four in the senior.

The seniors will go to the school on graduation. The juniors will be given a chance to qualify at this summer vacation.

Would 'Treat 'em Rough'

Four men stood outside the army recruiting office at Twelfth Street and Grand Avenue at 7:45 o'clock this morning when the sergeant opened up. A stout, red faced man wearing a khaki shirt was the first up the stairs.

"I'm the treat 'em rough man," he bawled. "That cat in the poster has nothing on me. Where do you join the tankers?"

"Have to wait for Lieutenant Cooter," said the sergeant. "He decides whether you'll treat 'em rough or not."

The fat man waited outside the door. By 9 o'clock thirty men crowded the third floor hallway. The stout man was nearest the door. Just behind him was a gray haired man wearing a derby, a well cut gray suit, a purple tie, socks to match and a silk handkerchief with a light purple border peeping from his vest pocket.

"I'm over draft age and it doesn't matter what my profession is," he said. "I never really wanted to get into this war before, but the tanks are different. I guess I can treat 'em rough."

The crowd grew steadily. By 10 o'clock there were forty applicants. Some of the men were humming, others talking among themselves. The stout man, perspiration pouring down his face, held his place next the door. He tried to whistle, but his lips wouldn't pucker. He stood on one foot, then the other. He mopped his face with a handkerchief, and finally bolted out through the crowd.

"He looked pretty hot but he got cold feet," a mechanic in overalls commented.

After the fat man left there was a slight exodus. A high school boy with a geometry book decided in favor of school. Two flashily dressed youths said, "Aw, let's get a beer." One man, saying nothing, slipped away.

Can't stand the gaff," said the mechanic.

But most of the applicants stayed. A youth wearing an army shirt explained: "It's my girl. I belonged to the home guards and she kind of kidded me. Nobody's going to kid a tanker, I guess."

The opinion of most of the men was voiced by a clerk. "I don't know anything about tractors or machinery, but I can learn to work a machine gun and I want to get across. Gee, I hope I get in."

A little man with double lens glasses said: "I don't suppose they'll take me. Guess I'm pretty useless. But I want to try. It's about my last chance. They all throw me down." When Lieut. Frank E. Cooter, special tank recruiting officer, appeared, the crowd formed a line outside the door. The men were admitted one at a time. Moistening their lips, they entered the little room and stated their qualifications.

John R. Ecklund, 27 years old, was one of the first admitted. "What mechanical experience have you had?" he was asked. "None. I'm an attorney for the Kansas City Street Railways Company," he replied.

"Why do you want to join?"

"I want to see action and get over in a hurry."

Lieutenant Cooter accepted him.

"That is the type of all of them," the lieutenant said. "That is what brings men here. Not promises of high pay or easy service, but telling the truth about quick action and danger. 'To know and yet to dare,' would be a good slogan. Quick service, quick promotion and action, action, is what brings them. They are the finest type of men for soldiers."

Besides Ecklund six other men were accepted for service up to noon.

Recruits for the Tanks

A line of men wound from the front room of the third floor of the Army recruiting station, Twelfth and Grand Avenue, through the hall and half way downstairs. Some of the men were jostling and laughing, others looked sober and looked thoughtfully at the posters on the wall. Mechanics in overalls, bookkeepers, stenographers, school teachers who would have difficulty with the physical examination, and athletic college students, all were in line.

The head of the line stopped at the door of a room where a freckled faced young second lieutenant sat at a desk. He nodded, a man was admitted, asked a few questions, sized up by the lieutenant and then either told he was not wanted or given a card to sign.

"It's the spirit of adventure which brings them up here," said Lieut. Frank E. Cooter, of the Tank Corps, the latest branch of the United States Army. "Every man in line there is a potential crusader. They may not have realized it until today. Then they came up to enlist. We do not offer anything easy. The tank corps is no place for those that want noncombatant jobs and desk soldiers needn't apply. But we guarantee quick action, active service, a good chance for a commission and adventure. The tank work is dangerous, of course, but men will always apply for clean, dangerous work with a chance for quick advancement."

More than fifty men applied at the recruiting office yesterday and Lieutenant Cooter recommended the enlistment of eighteen. Men of mechanical skill are wanted especially but an order from Col. I.C. Welborn, of the tank corps authorized Lieutenant Cooter to accept any men "qualified by soldierly qualities."

Arthur McKnight and Albert Findley, Kansas City newspapermen, enlisted in the new service yesterday. The other men enlisted ranged in occupation from truck drivers to school teachers. Letters and telegrams of application were received from all over the Middle West yesterday.

Daredevil Joins Tanks

"Have you ever had any gas engine experience?" asked Lieut. Frank E. Cooter, special tank officer at the army recruiting station, Twelfth Street and Grand Avenue, yesterday.

"Well, you might call it that," replied William A. Whitman, 914 East Ninth Street. "I've driven a Blitzen-Benz at the Chicago, New York, Cincinnati and Los Angeles speedways for the last four years. You might call my race with Ralph Mulford at Reno a gas engine experience. Or the time the old boat got up to 111 miles an hour at the Sheepshead Bay track, or when Bob Burman was killed on the big board oval and I piled up right behind him. Those were gas engine experiences."

"But have you had any military experience?" asked Lieutenant Cooter.

"Well, not regular military. I held a lieutenant's commission in the Nicaraugan army in the war against Honduras in 1909. I was also a machine gun captain with Madero when he put Diaz out. First American to get into Juarez. Ask Pancho Villa, he knows . But none of those were very military. I had a commission in a couple of Central American revolutions, too. Nothing very military there, either."

Lieutenant Cooter shoved a blank toward him. "Sign on the dotted line, man," he said. "You're too good to be true!"

"Well, I haven't raced since September at Sheepshead Bay, and I may be a little out of practice, but you don't have to go so fast in a tank. Besides, I've got a little difficulty with my teeth. But I sure want to sign for the tanks."

Lieutenant Cooter has wired Washington requesting waivers as to the teeth.

Besides the regular quota of mechanics, barbers, motor car salesmen, bartenders and college students who applied yesterday, Maynard Bush, 38 years old, instructor in journalism at Polytechnic Junior College, made out an application. He will not be enlisted until next week, so he may arrange for a successor.

Letters were received from several Kansas University students who wish to enter. The Sigma Alpha Epsilon Chapter at Manhattan, Kas., wrote that several of its members wished to enlist. Telegrams and letters came throughout yesterday in regard to the t ank service.

One hundred and sixteen men were accepted by Lieutenant Cooter during the week for immediate service. Nineteen were taken yesterday.

Mix War, Art and Dancing

Outside a woman walked along the wet street-lamp lit sidewalk through the sleet and snow.

Inside in the Fine Arts Institute on the sixth floor of the Y.W.C.A. Building, 1020 McGee Street, a merry crowd of soldiers from Camp Funston and Fort Leavenworth fox trotted and one-stepped with girls from the Fine Arts School while a sober faced you ng man pounded out the latest jazz music as he watched the moving figures. In a corner a private in the signal corps was discussing Whistler with a black haired girl who heartily agreed with him. The private had been a member of the art colony at Chicago before the war was declared.

Three men from Funston were wandering arm in arm along the wall looking at the exhibition of paintings by Kansas City artists. The piano player stopped. The dancers clapped and cheered and he swung into "The Long, Long Trail Awinding". An infantry corporal, dancing with a swift moving girl in a red dress, bent his head close to hers and confided something about a girl in Chautauqua, Kas. In the corridor a group of girls surrounded a tow-headed young artilleryman and applauded his imitation of his p al Bill challenging the colonel, who had forgotten the password. The music stopped again and the solemn pianist rose from his stool and walked out into the hall for a drink.

A crowd of men rushed up to the girl in the red dress to plead for the next dance. Outside the woman walked along the wet lamp lit sidewalk.

It was the first dance for soldiers to be given under the auspices of the War Camp Community Service. Forty girls of the art school, chaperoned by Miss Winifred Sexton, secretary of the school and Mrs. J. F. Binnie were the hostesses. The idea was formulated by J. P. Robertson of the War Camp Community Service, and announcements were sent to the commandants at Camp Funston and Fort Leavenworth inviting all soldiers on leave. Posters made by the girl students were put up at Leavenworth on the interurb an trains.

The first dance will be followed by others at various clubs and schools throughout the city according to Mr. Robertson.

The pianist took his seat again and the soldiers made a dash for partners. In the intermission the soldiers drank to the girls in fruit punch. The girl in red, surrounded by a crowd of men in olive drab, seated herself at the piano, the men and the gi rls gathered around and sang until midnight. The elevator had stopped running and so the jolly crowd bunched down the six flights of stairs and rushed waiting motor cars. After the last car had gone, the woman walked along the wet sidewalk through the sle et and looked up at the dark windows of the sixth floor.